THE COACHES' COLLECTION OF FIELD HOCKEY DRILLS

EDITED BY DONNA FONG
UNIVERSITY OF CALIFORNIA, BERKELEY

Leisure Press
P.O. Box 3
West Point, N.Y. 10996

A publication of Leisure Press.
P.O. Box 3, West Point, N.Y. 10996
Copyright © 1982 by Donna Fong
All rights reserved. Printed in the U.S.A.

ISBN 0-88011-040-6

Library of Congress Number: 81-86506

Text photographs by Richard Zoller
Cover photo: Richard Zoller
Cover design: Diana Goodin

Contents

Message From The Editor

The purpose of this book is to share with the reader the many drills that are used by the contributing coaches whose experiences range from international and national play, and coaching at high schools, colleges, private and national camps. All the drills are not originals. Several have been edited over and over again by many coaches from all parts of the world.

I strongly feel that the proper use of drills is very important to developing a successful team. How a coach approaches each drill, extrapolates the relevant and applies the concepts can make a critical difference in the results achieved on the field. Field hockey should be played with **skill**. Without a doubt, a coach can help her athletes acquire, practice and perfect those skills. Better to challenge the individuals of your team with a drill that you believe in rather than go through the motions without a specific purpose in mind.

The drills in this book have been divided into five categories: specific skills; intervals and circuits; goalkeeping and scoring; circle play; and small games. Each drill has a specific skill emphasis even though many of the drills share many skills in common. Hopefully, the index will help facilitate the selection of drills for the reader.

In conclusion I would like to thank the coaches who have contributed their ideas and thoughts concerning the game. Without their help, this book would not be possible. A special thanks to Richard Zoller who contributed his collection of fine photographs.

INDEX OF CONTRIBUTORS

INDEX OF DRILLS

PART I:

PART II:

PART III:

PART IV:

PART V:

PART I:
Specific Skills

DRILL #1
CUTTING

Emphasis: Cutting, receiving and passing.

Formation: Two players A and B. Sessions must be short to maintain intensity ($\pm$ 25 seconds). Confine players to approximately 20 X 20 yard area to start.

Procedure: A drives the ball to B. A accelerates in any direction with the stick showing where she wants the pass. B runs to meet the ball and immediately passes to A. B then makes her cut and asks for the ball.

Variation:
- One touch.
- Three people with one ball. Keep set passing rotation.

DRILL #2
CUT BACK

Emphasis: Cutting back to receive a pass.

Formation:

- - - - → Movement w/o ball   ∼∼∼→ Dribble
──────→ Pass   ⟩⟩⟩⟩⟩⟩ Shot

Procedure: Passer X_2 waits for X_1 to run forward to the cone and cut back to receive the pass. X_1 then dribbles towards the end line and centers the ball to X_2 who receives and shoots. X_3 rushes.

Variation:

- X_1 can pass to the top of the circle where X_2 is waiting for the ball to take a shot at goal.
- X_2 can cut into the circle and the pass goes back to X_3 who is waiting at the top to shoot.
- Add a defense so that X_1 must think about where to make the pass.
- Use the left side of the field.

DRILL #3
FIGURE EIGHT -
THREE PLAYER WEAVE

Emphasis: Passing, cutting to the ball, overload on the goalkeeper.

Formation:

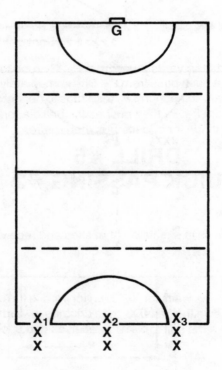

Procedure: The player in the middle may pass either right or left to begin the weave. The passer must remember to cut behind the player she passes to. The players continue the weave until they reach the striking circle. The player with the ball has the option to take the shot or to pass off to her teammate.

14

DRILL #4
QUICK PASSING #1

Emphasis: Quickness in execution of passes and receiving.

Formation:
➞ Pass
- - ➞ Movement w/o ball

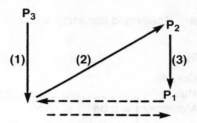

Procedure: P_1 starts ten yards away from P_2. P_1 runs to her left and receives a push pass from P_3. She immediately pushes the ball diagonally to her right. P_1 then runs to her right and receives a pass from P_2. P_1 then pushes the ball diagonally to her left to P_3. Continue for one minute, then rotate.

DRILL #5
QUICK PASSING #2

Emphasis: Quickness in execution of passes and receiving.

Formation:

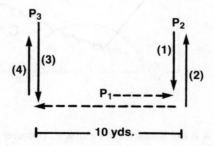

I————— 10 yds. —————I

Procedure: P_1 starts between P_2 and P_3. P_2 and P_3 have a ball. P_2 pushes the ball to P_1 who receives and pushes the ball back to P_2. P_1 then runs to her left and receives a push pass from P_3. P_1 returns the ball to P_3. Continue for one minute, then rotate.

DRILL #6
THREES PASSING

Emphasis: Agility and passing.

Formation:
~~~~► Dribble
———► Pass
– – –► Movement w/o ball

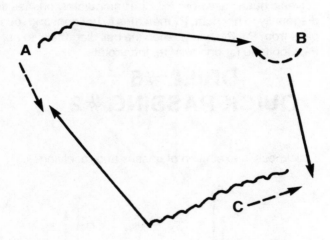

Procedure: A if necessary cuts back to receive the ball from C. Once A receives she carries the ball on a diagonal to her left for five steps and does a reverse stick pass to her right. B moves towards the ball and allows the ball to cross in front before she scoops a back pass to C. C gathers the ball and moves on a diagonal to A and flicks the ball to A. Rotate after five rounds.

DRILL #7
MOBILITY

Emphasis: Footwork, readiness in receiving, accuracy of hit.

Formation:

⟶ Hit
( ) Sequence
• Ball

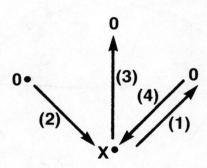

Procedure: Player X and one of the players O have a ball each. X always hits the ball to a free O. X after hitting the ball must be ready to receive the ball from one of the O players.

Variation: Use push passes only.

DRILL #8
THE EGG

Emphasis: Receiving and passing on the move.

Formation:

~~~► Dribble

---► Movement w/o ball

——► Pass

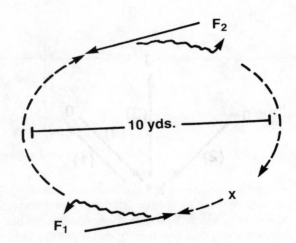

Procedure: X starts accelerating and receives a pass from F_1. X fields the ball cleanly and dribbles to a point opposite F_1. She passes to F_1 and repeats the same task. Continue interval for 1-1/2 to 2 minutes. X and F alternate.

Variation:
- Go both directions.
- No use of dribble.

DRILL #9
TOUCH AND SEND

Emphasis: Receiving in front and behind.

Formation:

△ Cone

━━━▶ Pass

〜〜〜▶ Dribble

- - - ▶ Movement w/o ball

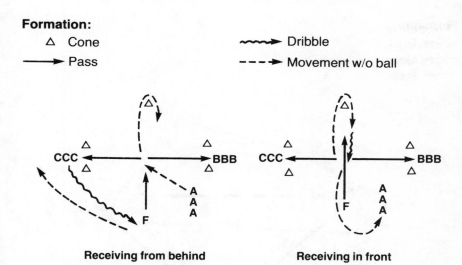

Receiving from behind   Receiving in front

Procedure: A cuts and receives the ball from the left rear. She passes immediately either right or left through the cones and sprints ahead around the cone. She then receives the ball in front and passes right or left and then goes behind the feeder to the end of the line. Players B or C after receiving the ball Indian dribble to the feeder, leave the ball and go to the end of the line. They should be running at top speed. The balls should be fed as quickly as possible to place maximum pressure on line A. After several turns, rotate. Goalkeepers may participate in pads at all stations.

Variation:
- Change direction and receive from the right.
- Two touch or one touch with the better players.
- Add stick fake one way and pass the opposite direction.

DRILL #10
GETTING AROUND THE BALL

Emphasis: Collecting from the right, hitting to the right.

Formation:

⟶ Pass

--➤ Movement w/o ball

  •   Ball

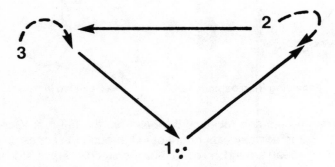

Procedure: Player one has three balls and passes in order as soon as player two has just enough time to get ready to come around the ball. Player three receives the ball and passes back to player one. Time should be minimized in execution to make the players work under pressure. After three passes, the players rotate positions.

Variation: • Player three can use a reverse stick back pass.

DRILL #11
STICK ON THE BALL

Emphasis: Improve reaction time, hand eye co-ordination, clearing.

Formation:
  X - Shooter
  D - Defender
 ⟩⟩⟩⟩ - Shot

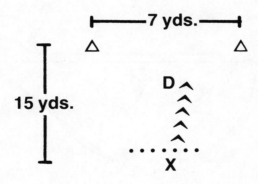

Procedure: X hits the ball alternately left and right but between the cones. The defender attempts to deflect the balls to prevent goals being scored. As soon as the defender touches the ball or if a goal is scored, the next shot is made.

Variation: • The defender attempts to field the ball cleanly and clears to the side she fielded the ball.

DRILL #12
WRIST IT IN

Emphasis: Footwork, use of wrists to get off quick flick or push.

Formation:
   G - Goalkeeper
   F - Shooter
   ⟶ Pass
   ⟩ ⟩ ⟩ Shot

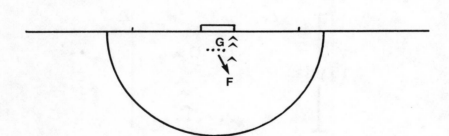

Procedure: The goalkeeper kicks the ball to the forward and she immediately aims for the corner of the goal. The shot must be either a flick or push. The goalkeeper may kick the ball to the right or left of the forward. The forward shoots for one minute.

Variation: ● Extend the time for conditioning purposes.

22

DRILL #13
GIVE AND GO

Emphasis: Accurate hitting, acceleration, change of direction.

Formation:
——► Pass
--→ Movement w/o ball
( ) Sequence

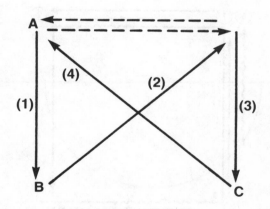

Procedure: B and C station themselves at the corners of the grid. A shuttles the other two corners. A passes to B and moves to the opposite corner to get the return pass from B. A hits to C. A runs to the opposite corner to get the return pass from C. Note: A should not run until the hitter is prepared to hit.

Variation: ● Create more pressure on A by speeding up the hits.
● Use variation of strokes.

DRILL #14
AROUND THE SQUARE

Emphasis: Hitting and receiving.

Formation:

⟶ Pass
--➤ Movement w/o ball
~~➤ Dribble

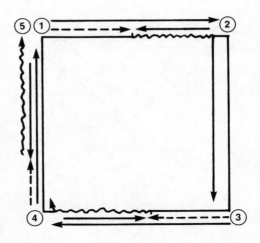

Procedure:
- 1 hits to 2. 2 hits back to 1 who moves towards the ball. 1 hits a square pass across to 3.
- 3 receives the pass with the reverse stick and immediately hits to 4. 4 returns hit to 3 who meets the ball and then sends a reverse pass to 4.
- 4 hits to 5. 5 returns the hit to 4 who meets the ball and sends a reverse pass to 5.
- Continue with all players having rotated clockwise.

DRILL #15
REACH

Emphasis: Acceleration, reaching to field the ball, passing quickly.

Formation:
- - -▶ Movement w/o ball
~~▶ Dribble
───▶ Pass

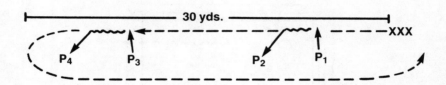

Procedure: X runs along the line at full speed. The ball is passed by passer 1 so that X must reach at full extension to prevent the ball from going out. After collecting the ball, X passes to P_2. X accelerates to receive the ball from passer 3 who passes so that X must reach at full extension to field the ball. After collecting the ball, she passes to P_4 and returns back to the line. Next X player may start as soon as the first pass reaches P_2.

Variation: ● Reverse directions.
● Vary placement of pass.
● Include a dodge after X receives the pass.

DRILL #16
ONE HAND SKILL

Emphasis: Improve one's reach, enable the person with possession of the ball to run faster with the ball in an open field situation.

Formation:

~~~► Dribble

• Ball

1. X₂ X₁  X₃

2. X₂ X₁ 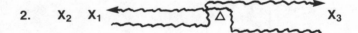 X₃

Procedure:
- X₁ player dribbles only with the stick in her right hand until she gets to X₃. X₃ dribbles to the opposite side only with the stick held in her left hand. Vary the angle of the arm in relationship to one's side (45° to 90°).
- X₁ dribbles the ball with her right hand only and pulls the ball to her left as she approaches the cone. She then dribbles the ball with her left hand until she gets to X₃. X₃ repeats the drill but starts with her left hand to dribble the ball, pulls left and continues dribbling the ball with the right hand only.

DRILL #17
GO FOR THE CONES

Emphasis: Change of direction, acceleration, fakes.

Formation:

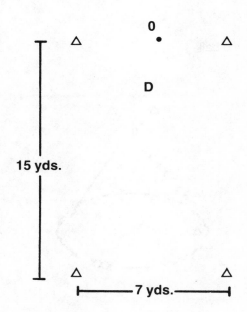

Procedure: Player O's goal is to try and move the ball past the defense and score by touching either cone with the ball. If successful, she immediately changes direction and continues until the defense can get possession of the ball. The defense then becomes the attacking player, the attacking player, the defense. Time limit of two to three minutes.

DRILL #18
HIT AND MOVEMENT OFF BALL

Emphasis: Hitting for accuracy, positioning for receiving.

Formation:

△ △ Goals
——➤ Pass
〰〰➤ Dribble
〉〉〉〉 Shot
——➤ Movement w/o ball

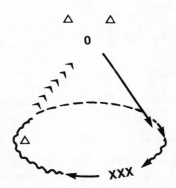

Procedure: X pushes the ball to a space in front of her, collects the ball and quickly goes around the cone and gets a quick hit off. X then cuts over to her right and gets into position to receive a pass from O. She dribbles back to the starting point.

Variation: • Have the players move the opposite direction so that the cut is to the left.

28

DRILL #19
BEATING AN OPPONENT

Emphasis: Timing of dodge, awareness of teammate's positioning.

Formation:

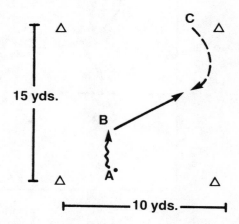

Procedure: Player A starts with the ball and moves forward to dodge B who is advancing. On successful completion of the dodge, A passes to C who moves into position to receive. C must move from her starting point in order to receive. On receiving the ball, C and A change roles and B remains as the defender. If player A is not successful in beating B, she starts again from the starting point.

Variation: • C could return the ball to A with a drive which would add receiving to A's task.
  • Time the drill and make it an interval drill.
  • Change the stroke to be used.

DRILL #20
ALL PURPOSE

Emphasis: Wing play with interchange, fast break, shot on goal with rush, goalkeeping.

Formation:

⟶ Pass
∿➤ Dribble
--➤ Movement w/o ball
≫≫ Shot

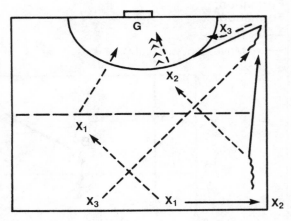

Procedure:
- Ball starts with X_1. X_1 passes to X_2 and moves off the ball and cuts diagonally left downfield to fill the lane vacated by X_3. Eventually she will back up the centering pass from X_3. X_2 receives the ball at the sideline and carries it until X_3 is in position. X_2 passes to the corner (angled so if the ball is not received, it will go out of bounds on the side line). Immediately after passing the ball X_2 cuts diagonally left to just outside the circle to receive the centered pass from X_3. X_2 receives the pass and shoots.
- X_3 makes a strong diagonal sprint to the right corner flag to receive the pass from X_2. The sprint should be started as the pass is made from X_1 to X_2. If necessary the ball is taken to the end line as X_2 moves into position to receive a diagonal pass back to the top of the circle.
- As the shot is made all players move into rushing and circle play positions. Play the ball until it is out of the circle.

DRILL #21
THREE PLAYER THROUGH PASSING

Emphasis: Quick penetration of defense, interchanging of positions by forwards.

Formation:

⟶ Pass

⟶ Movement w/o ball

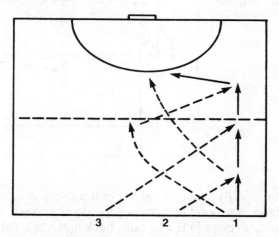

Procedure: Players 1, 2, and 3 line up at the fifty yard line about ten yards apart. 1 makes a through pass to 2 who makes a diagonal cut to pick up the ball. 1 cuts diagonally left to 3's position. 2 makes the through pass to 3 who cuts for the pass. 2 then cuts back to the left. 3 makes a flat pass across the circle and 1 or 2 attempt to control the pass and shoot for goal.

Variation:
- The drill can be timed from the first pass to shot on goal.
- Add defense at the top of the circle.
- The flat pass could be a pass across the goal mouth giving the forwards an opportunity to practice deflections.

DRILL #22
DODGE CITY

Emphasis: Possession dodges.

Formation:

  G - Goalkeeper
  F - Feeder
  ——▶ Pass
  ---▶ Movement w/o ball
  〰▶ Dribble
  △△ Cones

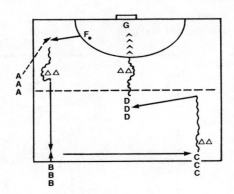

Procedure: Feeder (F) passes wide out of the circle. A cuts back to re-ceive in support and dodges the double cones. She sends a through pass to B who pulls back and hits a flat pass to her right. C picks up the flat ball, executes a dodge and accel-erates downfield. At the twenty-five yard line C passes back to D who collects the ball at full speed, executes a dodge at the cones and takes a shot on goal.

Note: Emphasize that possession dodges are to be used. Each player should take three to four consecutive turns be-fore rotating.

Variation:
- Add body or stick fakes prior to each dodge or pass.
- For more pressure, add a defender in place of the double cones.

DRILL #23
RECOVERY TACKLE PROGRESSION

Emphasis: Controlled stealing the ball with purpose.

Formation:

--► Movement w/o ball
──► Pass
〜〜► Dribble
• Ball

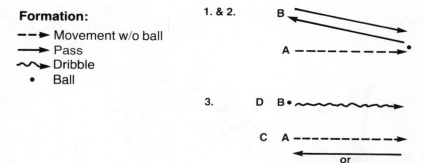

Procedure:
- A sprints to the ball. Just before pulling it toward the body she looks at her partner B who is holding up a number (1-5). A must call the number before pulling the ball. A then passes to B, B passes back to A who replaces the stationary ball. Players then exchange roles.
- If B holds up an even number, A dribbles after pulling the ball; if B holds up an odd number, A passes.
- With four players A, B, C, and D, A and C are teammates; B and D likewise. One ball is used. A and B are back to back with C and D. B dribbles the ball. A runs on the right or left of B and just before stealing the ball must look at C who shows a number (1-5). If an even number is shown, A dribbles back to C; if odd, A passes to C. Then C dribbles for D to steal while B shows a number. The first five trials use a passive dribble; the next five the dribbler attempts to maintain possession.

  Note: Proper technique should be taught for left and right approach to the ball prior to step 1. Repeat each step ten trials before moving to the next. Complete all phases before approaching the ball from the other side. Instead of number, the cue could be a stick in different positions.

DRILL #24
ICE CREAM

Emphasis: Quick reaction shots on loose balls in front of the goal.

Formation:

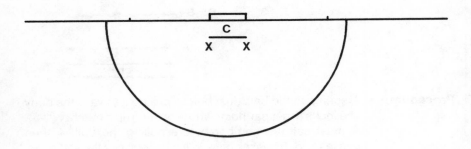

Procedure: The coach uses a large bucket of balls (15-20).
Set a barrier (5-6 feet wide) in front of the coach and about five yards in front of the goal mouth. Set up two players one to two yards from the barrier. Coach randomly tosses balls in front of the barrier as fast as possible. The two players must shoot and/or move the ball and shoot as quickly as possible. Shots must go around the barrier, not over it.

Variation:
- One player at a time does the drill.
- Dump the entire bucket of balls at once and each player gets as many balls into the cage as possible.

DRILL #25
2 v 2

Emphasis: The defense working together to prevent a pass being made behind them.

Formation:

A_1 B - Attacking players
D_1 D_2 - Defensive players
➖➤ - Movement w/o Ball
➡ - Pass

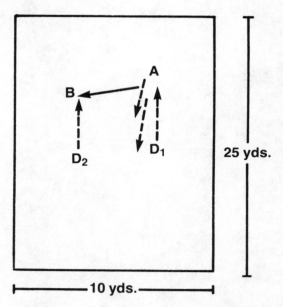

25 yds.

10 yds.

Procedure: D_1 closes the gap to make a tackle. D_2 does not commit herself to going forward until she is sure that the ball is going to B. The moment D_2 moves forward to put pressure on B, D_1 moves backward to prevent B from returning the ball behind D_1 to A. At the beginning of the drill, A and B can be limited to just square passes. Eventually, they can be given various passes to use.

PART II:
Conditioning, Intervals, Circuits

DRILL #26
CONTINUOUS SLALOM

Emphasis: Individual stickwork and ball control.

Formation:

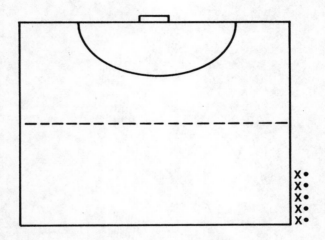

Procedure: Each person with a ball lines up in file formation. The first person in line begins weaving through the line using the Indian dribble and incorporating stick and body fakes. When she passes two people, the next person in line begins her weaving. As the players reach the end of the line, they become posts until it is their turn again.

Variation:
- Split the group in half and have a race around the field.
- Time the whole team at various times of the season and see if there is improvement.

DRILL #27
PASS AND GO

Emphasis: Interval training with 1 v 1, passing and shooting.

Formation:
⟶ Pass
⟿ Dribble
--→ Movement w/o ball

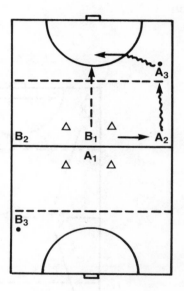

Procedure: A_1 and B_1 begin with 1 v 1 in the middle of the field. The winner immediately passes the ball to 2 who is in the right wing position. As soon as 1 passes to 2, she runs towards goal. 3 who has a ball dribbles towards goal and either passes to 1 or shoots. After 2 receives the ball from 1, she indian dribbles to the twenty-five yard line and becomes a 3. 3 becomes 1, 1 becomes 2 and the drill is repeated.

Variation:
● Time the drill.
● Use the left wing as 2.
● Add a defensive player in the circle.

DRILL #28
HOURGLASS

Emphasis: Conditioning and passing.

Formation:
⟶ Hit
• Ball

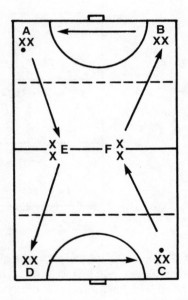

Procedure: Two players are stationed at A, B, C, D, E, F. Drill begins at A and C with the players having the ball. The player at A hits to E and runs to E. Likewise, C hits to F and runs to F. The players at E and F receive the hit and send the ball on to the next station. The players who just hit must remember to follow their hit to the next station. Continue the drill for a designated time.

DRILL #29
SHUTTLE RUN

Emphasis: Conditioning, agility, quickness, body control.

Formation:

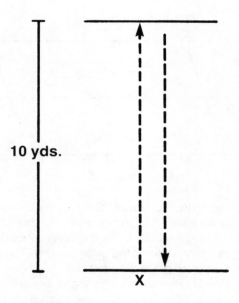

10 yds.

X

Procedure: Each ten yard run is one repetition. Complete ten repetitions. Repetitions one to five. Run forward to the line and return running backwards. At each line the person must touch the line with her stick flat to the ground. Repetitions six to ten. Run up and back but alternate direction in which the player turns each time.

Variation: ● Add the use of the ball for ball control work.

DRILL #30
CONCENTRATED STICKWORK

Emphasis: Stickwork control.

Formation:

→ Pass
- -► Dribble
- Ball

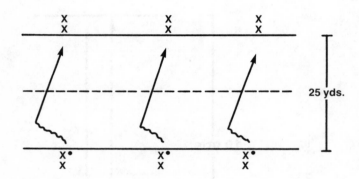

Procedure: Have no more than four or five players to a group. The fewer, the harder each individual must work. The drill begins with the coach giving the task. Once the task is completed, the individual goes to the end of the opposite line. The drill is continued until the coach gives the next task.

Example of tasks within a period of ten to fifteen minutes:

- Indian dribble, pulling left and push pass before the dotted line.
- Two quick taps left, reverse, push pass before the line.
- Swerve dribble twenty-five yards and finish with a reverse square pass to the next person who will do the task going the opposite direction.
- The same as above except emphasize change of pace and acceleration.
- Dribble ahead, fake swerve right and pull left, finish with reverse square pass.
- Push ball left, pull back with the reverse stick reach, finish with push to the right.

DRILL #31
FULL FIELD SPEEDWORK WITH BALL

Emphasis: Conditioning and ball control.

Formation:

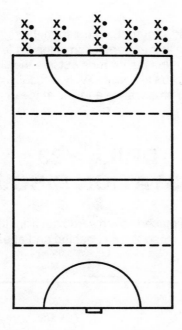

Procedure:
- Indian dribble to the twenty-five yard line.
- Zig zag dribble (no use of reverse stick) to the fifty yard line.
- Speed dribble to the end line. Put the ball ahead three yards when there is an open field.
- Rest.
- Repeat.

DRILL #32
FOUR STATION CIRCUIT - 1

Emphasis: Maximum activity which utilizes speed, quickness, agility, footwork, stickwork.

Formation:

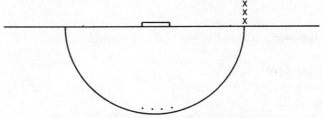

Procedure: Timed and scored. Execute from the right side as well as the left. Begin at the intersection of the circle and end line. On the signal "go" the player runs outside the circle and drives each of the four balls successively at goal. The clock stops when the player crosses the end line at the opposite side.

DRILL #33
FOUR STATION CIRCUIT - 2

Formation: A cone is placed seven yards out from the center of the goal. A ball is placed in front, behind and at each side of the cone.

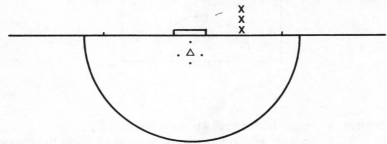

Procedure: A player starts from the end line and collects a ball, dribbles the ball to the sixteen yard line and executes a shot at goal. She returns to the cone area and repeats the drill again until all of the balls have been hit at goal. The clock stops when the last ball crosses the end line.

DRILL #34
FOUR STATION CIRCUIT - 3

Emphasis:

Formation:

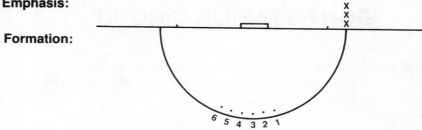

Procedure: Timed and scored. Can be done from both sides. The player begins at the intersection of the circle and the end line. The player goes to ball two and hits; she then goes back to ball one and hits. She repeats this pattern until all the balls are hit. The clock stops when the player crosses the end line on the opposite side of the circle.

DRILL #35
FOUR STATION CIRCUIT - 4

Emphasis:

Formation:

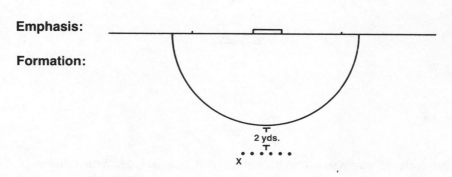

Procedure: Timed in sixty seconds. The trials are done from right and left side. On the signal "go" the player dribbles any ball to the designated line (top of the circle) and takes a quick shot at goal. She then runs back to the next ball and repeats the same task until all the balls have been hit or the time is up.

DRILL #36
EIGHT STATION CIRCUIT - 1

Emphasis: Variety of basic skills put in a pressure situation.
Eight stations of eight teams with three players on each team.

Formation:
~~~► Dribble

Procedure: Weave up and back through the cones. Count the number of cones dribbled around during the one minute.

Note: Have a reliable timer who blows the whistle to start and stop each drill. Six minutes are allowed for each station which allows each individual to do the drill twice. The captain of each team keeps a running score from station to station.

DRILL #37
EIGHT STATION CIRCUIT - 2

Emphasis:

Formation:

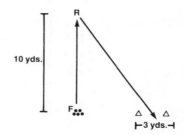

Procedure: Receive the ball from the feeder and pass the ball back between the cones. The next ball cannot be received until the ball has been sent through the cones. If the pass does not go between the cones, the receiver must retrieve the ball and pass it through the cones.

DRILL #38
EIGHT STATION CIRCUIT - 3

Emphasis:

Formation:

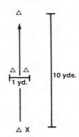

Procedure: Pass the ball to the opposite cone and sprint to receive the pass. The ball and the player should arrive at the same time. Continue until one minute is up. The cones should be one yard apart. Each pass must go through the set of cones and must reach the end cone in order to score a point. Time limit is one minute.

48

DRILL #39
EIGHT STATION CIRCUIT - 4

Emphasis:

Formation:

Procedure: Aerial dribble for one minute. The goal is to see how many continuous dribbles a player can do without missing.

DRILL #40
EIGHT STATION CIRCUIT - 5

Emphasis:

Formation:
∿► Dribble
──► Hit
--► Movement w/o ball

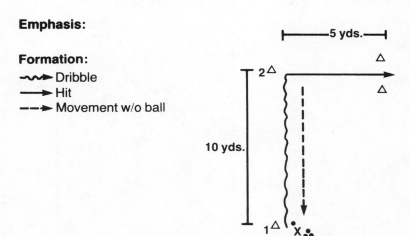

Procedure: The player begins behind cone 1. She dribbles to cone 2 and then reverse hits through cones 3 and 4. She runs back to cone 1 and repeats the drill. Time limit is one minute. Score the number of balls which go through cones 3 and 4.

DRILL #41
EIGHT STATION CIRCUIT - 6

Emphasis:

Formation:

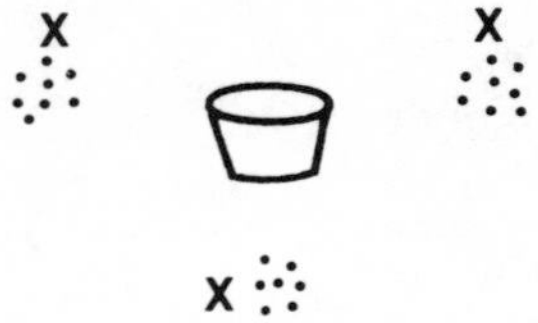

Procedure: Place a weighted bucket in the center of a six foot radius circle. The players try to scoop as many balls into the bucket in one minute.
Note: Make sure you have enough balls or have retrievers.

DRILL #42
EIGHT STATION CIRCUIT - 7

Emphasis:

Formation:

Procedure: The player dribbles the ball in a straight line and uses her footwork and hip swerve to get around the cones. The player tries to swerve around as many cones as possible for a score. Time limit of one minute.

DRILL #43
EIGHT STATION CIRCUIT - 8

Emphasis:

Formation:
    G - Goalkeeper
    X - Shooter
    ⌇⌇➤ Dribble
    〉〉〉〉 Shot
    • Ball

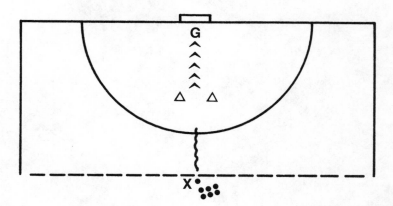

Procedure: The player dribbles from the twenty-five yard line to the edge of the circle and before reaching the cones takes a shot on goal. She immediately runs back to the twenty-five yard line and repeats the drill. Scoring is five points for a goal, three for a shot saved by the goalkeeper, zero for a missed shot at goal. Time limit of one minute.

PART III:
Goalkeeping and Shooting

DRILL #44
GOALKEEPER'S REBOUND DRILL

Emphasis: Handling a hard shot and clearing if possible, recovering quickly to opposite side of the cage to handle a follow up shot.

Formation:
- **G** - Goalkeeper
- **C** - Coach
- **X** - Hitter
- 〉〉〉〉 Shot at goal
- • Ball

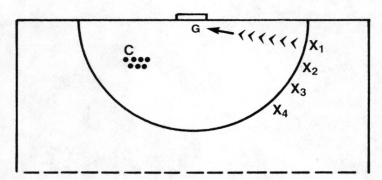

Procedure: X_1 hits the ball hard at goal. Coach (C); follows immediately with an underhand throw. (C) should challenge the goalie but make some of the tosses somewhat easy to give the goalkeeper confidence. The next X player prepares to shoot but she must wait until the goalkeeper quickly recovers to her post. Recovery to this post is very important in order to prevent a nearside goal.

Variation: • Change sides. Ten balls are enough for one side at a time. This is a good interval drill for the goalkeeper.

DRILL #45
OFF BALL CIRCLE DEFENSE

Emphasis: Defender working on recovery, communication with the goal-keeper.

Formation:
- **F -** Forwards
- **D -** Defense
- **G -** Goalkeeper
- ∿➤ Dribble
- --➤ Movement w/o ball
- ➝ Pass
- • Ball

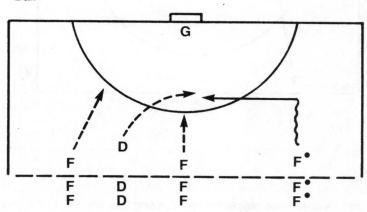

Procedure:
- Side forward carries the ball towards the circle and centers the ball.
- Goalkeeper covers the ball carrier.
- The defender recovers and positions to cover two forwards.
- The defender must position goal side to take the forward moving towards the ball and be able to cover the other forward if necessary.
- The defender must recover to assist in the clear if needed.

DRILL #46
GOALKEEPER'S SHIP

Emphasis: Goalkeeper communicating with her defense.

Formation:

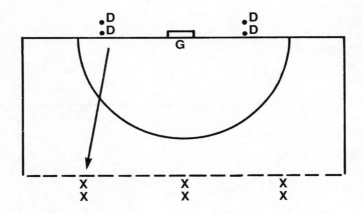

Procedure: A defensive player behind the end line hits the ball to one of the attacking players who must wait until the ball crosses the twenty-five yard line. The attacking players try to get the ball into the circle as fast as possible and try to get a shot at goal. The defensive player tries to put pressure on the ball and if the goalkeeper calls for the shot, she does not interfere. If the goalkeeper moves away from the mouth of the goal, the defensive player covers. Play continues until the ball is cleared, hit over the end line or crosses the goal line. Alternate sides on the initial hit from the defense.

DRILL #47
1 v 1 WITH THE GOALKEEPER

Emphasis: Goalkeeper concentrates on covering the angle.

Formation:

   G - Goalkeeper
   X - Shooter
   1-4 Feeders
   ● - Ball
   ——▶ Pass
   --▶ Movement w/o ball
  〉〉〉〉〉 Shot

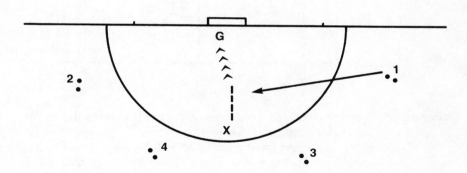

Procedure: X is the player shooting. X tries to get to the starting position after each shot is made from the designated stations. The goalkeeper has to remember where the next ball is coming from and position correctly. She must judge whether to go for the interception, position for the shot or try for the tackle.

DRILL #48
GOALKEEPER'S MOBILITY

Emphasis: Mobility, angle coverage, readiness for shot.

Formation:
- **G** - Goalkeeper
- **X** - Forwards
- **●** - Ball
- ---▶ Movement w/o ball
- ∿∿▶ Dribble
- ——▶ Pass
- ⟫⟫⟫⟫ Shot

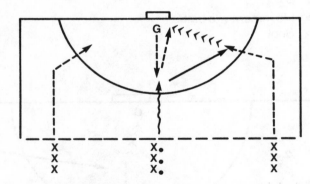

Procedure: Three attacking players move with speed towards the circle. The middle attacking player dribbles the ball just past the top of the circle and must pass to one of the other players who immediately takes a shot at goal. The goalkeeper must challenge the middle player and then immediately drop back as fast as possible to cover the angle and also be in readiness for the shot. Play continues until a score is made, the ball is hit out of bounds, or the ball is cleared out of the circle by the goalkeeper.

Note: The two side attacking players should stay wide so as to allow the goalkeeper time to drop back.

Variation: ● Allow the middle player to take a shot at goal.

58

DRILL #49
SHOOTING INTERVAL 1

Emphasis: Receiving and quick accurate shots at goal.

Formation:

  G - Goalkeeper
  X - Shooter
  P - Passer
––► Movement w/o ball

∿∿► Dribble
——► Pass
>>>>> Shot

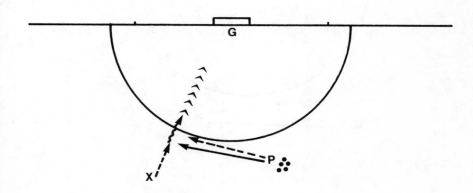

Procedure: X receives a pass just outside the circle and carries to just inside to shoot at goal. X then sprints back to the starting position to receive the next pass. X takes five shots. X should not chase poor passes. P the passer must be accurate and put the pressure on the player X.

Variation: ● Do the drill from the opposite side.

DRILL #50
SHOOTING INTERVAL 2

Emphasis:

Formation:

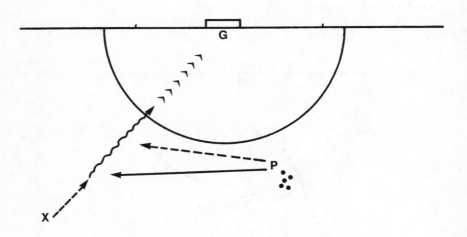

Procedure: Player X moves from the twenty-five yard line and receives the ball midway between the twenty-five yard line and the circle. She quickly moves towards the circle and shoots. Player X then must sprint back to the starting position and takes another turn. After five shots at goal, player X rests. Player P after each pass must put pressure on player X.

DRILL #51
SHOOTING INTERVAL 3

Emphasis: Redirecting a centered pass.

Formation:

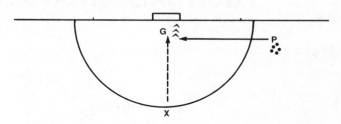

Procedure: Player X starts near the edge of the circle and sprints towards the goal to redirect the centered ball into the goal. Player X takes five turns and then rests.
Note: X player must run back to the starting point after each hit.

Variation: ● Start the drill without a goalkeeper. Later, add the goalkeeper.

DRILL #52
OFFENSE - DEFENSE CIRCLE PLAY

Emphasis: Quickness in shots at goal, footwork.

Formation:

X   Shooter
--→   Movement w/o ball
〉〉〉〉 Shot
●   Ball

Procedure: Player X runs to any ball and shoots immediately. She continues until all the balls are shot at goal.

Variation: ● Add defense so that it becomes a 1 v 1 situation.
● Add a goalkeeper.
● Incorporate a fake before the shot is made.

DRILL #53
FOUR BALL SHOOTING

Emphasis: Shooting, rushing, goalkeeping.

Formation:

G - Goalkeeper
c - Coach
x₁ Shooter
P - Passer

→ Pass
〰➤ Dribble
--➤ Movement w/o ball
⟩⟩⟩⟩⟩ Shot
• Ball

Procedure: Passer sends the ball to X_1 who is five yards outside the circle. X_1 receives and dribbles to the circle edge, shoots and rushes the shot on goal. X_1 and the goalkeeper play the ball until it is outside the circle. Once outside, the coach tosses another ball into a new playing area in the circle about ten yards from the goal line. Shooter and goalkeeper immediately reposition to the new ball. Shooter must then take the shot from the position where she fields the ball. The coach continues to toss balls into the shooting area (as balls go out of the circle) until a total of four balls are played by each shooter and goalkeeper. Repeat the above for a new shooter and new goalkeeper.

Variation: ● Allow player to dribble and draw the goalkeeper.
● Add a defensive player.

DRILL #54
WAVE

Emphasis: Rushing goal, keeping stick down, concentrating on the ball, repositioning.

Formation:

G - Goalkeeper   – – –► Movement w/o ball
F - Feeder   ──► Pass
X - Forwards   ›››› Shot
                      • Ball

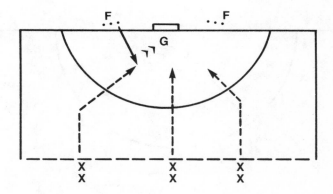

Procedure: A line of three players move toward the circle as the ball is rolled from the left or right side. After the shot is made at goal the players position for the ball coming off the pads. Once the play is finished, the players reposition for the next ball. The balls may come from the same side or may be alternated. Each group goes for three to six balls.

DRILL #55
THE SCORING TOUCH

Emphasis: Hand eye co-ordination.

Formation:

X_1 Shooter
X_2 Deflector
>>>> Shot

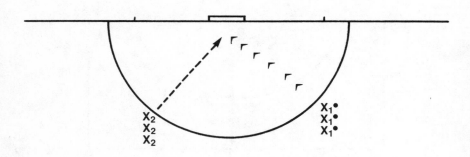

Procedure: X_1 dribbles the ball into the circle and immediately takes a shot at goal. X_1 must aim for the far post. X_2 must touch or deflect the ball into the goal even though the ball will go between the posts.

Variation: • Add a goalkeeper.
• Take the hit from the left.

DRILL #56
SEVEN BALL SHOOT

Emphasis: Quickness and accuracy of shots at goal, footwork.

Formation:

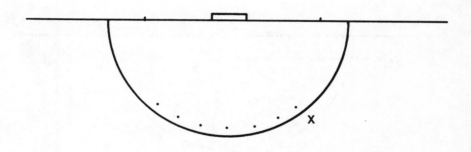

Procedure: On a signal from the coach the player begins at the far right and drives each ball towards the goal. This drill is timed.
Note: Have one player retrieving balls and another resetting the balls as the shooter moves along. This facilitates a quick changeover from one player to the next.

Variation:
- Place a cone to the left of each ball and make the player dribble the ball around the cone (moving left).
- Move balls outside of circle. Player dribbles in and hits on the run.

DRILL #57
DEFLECTION

Emphasis: Deflecting the ball into the goal.

Formation:

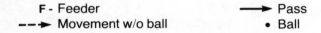

F - Feeder   ➜ Pass
‑‑➤ Movement w/o ball   • Ball

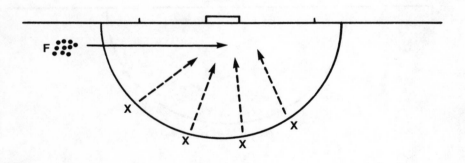

Procedure: Feeding player near the end line drives the ball across the mouth of the goal. Four players from the edge of the circle attempt to deflect the ball into the goal. They reposition and the drill is repeated.

Variation: • Work the ball across from the opposite side.

DRILL #58
WAVE

Emphasis: Hitting the pads, covering the posts, deflecting, repositioning.

Formation:

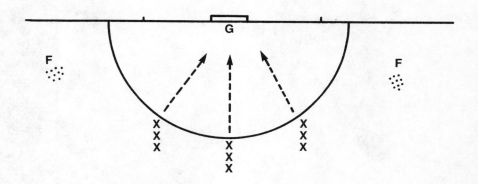

Procedure: Each feeder (F) has ten balls. Beginning on one side, the F sends a flat pass across the goal. The three X players rush and try to deflect the ball into the goal. They must also concentrate on covering the posts, hitting the pads. After the shot the X players must recover back for the next cross pass by back stepping and not by turning around. X players must stagger their "wave" to goal and not get caught flat. Drill continues with the next set of X players.

Variation: • Add one defender to cover the X player closest to the ball.

PART IV:
Circle Play

DRILL #59
3 v 3 CIRCLE PLAY

Emphasis: Defensive marking and clearing from the circle.
Tight offensive movement and passing into a space.

Formation:
G - Goalkeeper
X - Defense
O - Offense

P - Passer
• Ball

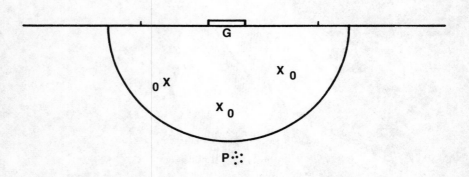

Procedure: P may only pass the ball. Play is continuous for approximately three minutes. Rotate positions.

Variation:
- Add a sweeper.
- Add that the passer may shoot. Stress that the sweeper must pick up the free player at the top of the circle.
- Add that the defense must get the ball to the twenty-five yard line. Stress the transition.

70

DRILL #60
MARKING

Emphasis: Marking.

Formation:

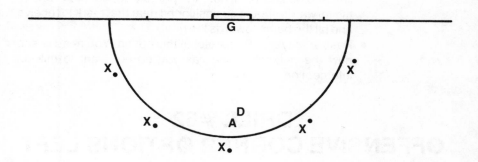

Procedure: Everyone has a ball at the edge of the circle. Two people are in the striking circle, one attacker and one defender. The drill begins when the coach calls a name. The person whose name is called passes to the attacker. The defender tries to mark and not allow the attacker to touch the ball. If the attacker gets possession of the ball, she takes a shot at goal or causes the defender to foul. If the defender gets possession of the ball, she clears the ball out of the circle. Once the ball is cleared or goes out of bounds, the coach calls another name. Switch players after four or five balls have been played.

Variation:
- Players on the edge of the circle may shoot or pass.
- Use more than one attacker, defender.

DRILL #61
OFFENSIVE CORNER OPTIONS RIGHT

Emphasis: Execution   **Formation:**

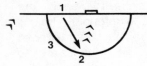

Option 1	Option 2	Option 3

Procedure: Player 2 who is receiving the corner hit has three options:
- Take the hit.
- Return the ball to player one who takes the ball to the end line and passes back near the penalty stroke mark. One of the forwards should be positioned near that mark to receive and hit the ball in towards the goal.
- Pass to player 3. Be careful of this option. You need to see how the defense rushes as you do not want to risk an interception.

DRILL #62
OFFENSIVE CORNER OPTIONS LEFT

Emphasis: Execution   **Formation:**

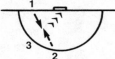

Option 1	Option 2	Option 3

Procedure: Player 2 who is receiving the corner hit has three options:
- Take the direct shot at goal.
- Pass to player 3 who first times the ball to the right side of the goal.
- Cut in for the hit and flick to the right side of the goal.

Note: The variation of corners keeps the defense guessing and off balance. Unless you have a sure hitter who never misses and scores a lot, try various plays.

DRILL #63
CIRCLE PLAY

Emphasis: Offense - Keep feet facing the goal, scoring off the rebound.
Defense - Marking, clearing.

Formation:

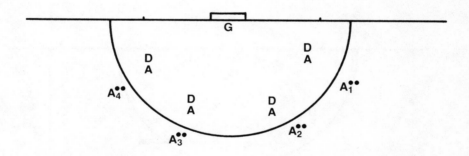

Procedure: The attack players at the edge of the circle take a shot on command. The defense marks a player and attempt to clear the ball from the circle. The attack tries to score from a deflection from the goalkeeper or defender or from a weak clear. Play ends when the ball leaves the circle. The next attack on the edge of the circle then shoots.

Variation: • Add more offense in the circle so that the defense must shift and mark the most dangerous players.

DRILL #64
4 v 3

Emphasis: Passing to the free player, marking, shooting, rushing.

Formation:

G - Goalkeeper	⟶	Pass
D - Defense	- - ▸	Movement w/o ball
F - Forwards	⟩⟩⟩⟩	Shot
P - Passer	•	Ball

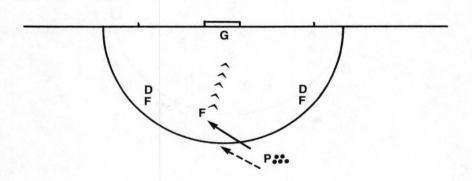

Procedure: The defense are assigned to mark a forward. The passer hits the ball to the free player who should be able to shoot. Forwards rush except the passer who advances to the top of the circle to pick up clears, feed the free player or takes a shot at goal. Play continues until a goal is made or the ball is cleared out of the circle. Repeat four times, then change players.

Variation: ● Start the forwards bunched and then have them move away from the free player to give her space for the shot at goal.

DRILL #65
GIVE AND GO

Emphasis: Recognize the "give and go" situation. Using acceleration to beat the defense.

Formation:

⟶ Pass   ⟩⟩⟩ Shot
- - ▶ Movement w/o ball

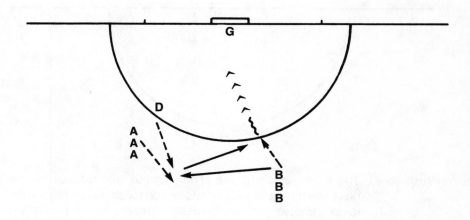

Procedure: A cuts back to receive a pass from B. A immediately first times the pass back to B who takes the shot at goal. B can choose to return a back door pass to A if the defense is anxious to intercept the first pass.

DRILL #66
DEFENSIVE COMMUNICATION

Emphasis: The goalkeeper needs to be assertive. The defense go for the rebounds and clear as quickly as possible.

Formation:

G - Goalkeeper   ---► Movement w/o ball
H - Hitter   ›››› Shot
D - Defense   • Ball

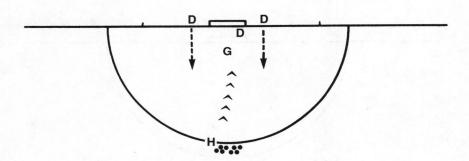

Procedure: The hitter yells "go" and simulates the time it takes for the ball to be hit in a regular offensive corner situation. Hitter then takes a shot at goal and the defense reacts. Do a series of ten to fifteen shots before rotating.

Note: This corner situation is just an example. Use your personnel according to their strengths. Make adjustments to weaknesses, i.e., goalkeeper split save to her left.

Variation: • Once the defense feels comfortable and confident of her job, work against the offense. Gradually add the other necessary players.

DRILL #67
2 v 1

Emphasis: Offense - Geting a shot at goal.
Defense - Forcing the ball handler wide and making the tackle.

Formation:

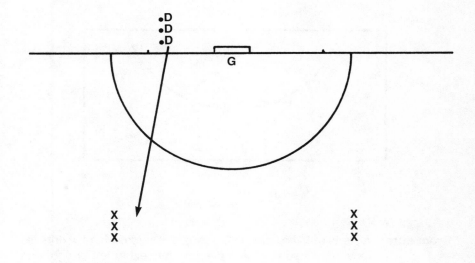

Procedure: The defense hits the ball to the offense and follows her pass. Offense goes 2 v 1 against the defense.

Variation: • 2 v 2 and have the defense coming from both sides of the goal.

DRILL #68
THINKING

Emphasis: Creating space, drawing the defense.

Formation:

   G - Goalkeeper   ⟶ Pass
  A, B - Offensive Players   ⟩⟩⟩⟩ Shot
  〰️⟶ Dribble

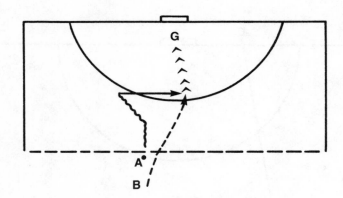

Procedure: A starts with the ball with B a couple of yards behind. A dribbles forward. As soon as A moves, B cuts either left or right and asks for a square pass. When A sees B, she must dribble on a diagonal away from B, then give the pass to her at the top of the circle. B first times the ball at goal. A and B continue to play until the ball is cleared or hit over the end line. Drill continues with another set of attacking players.

Variation: • Add a defense who starts on top of the circle and pressures A until the play is finished.
       • Defense can go to either player or to the space.

DRILL #69
GO FOR THE BALL

Emphasis: Anticipation.

Formation:

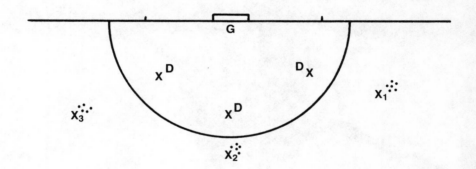

Procedure: Feeders X_1, X_2, X_3 alternate hitting hard hits into the circle to X player or directly at goal. X's try to get free to receive and shoot and to react to the ball coming off the pads. The defense concentrates on marking, intercepting and clearing. Play continues until the ball is out of the circle, over the end line or between the posts. The feeders should allow enough time between hits for the defense to mark properly according to the position of the ball.

Variation:
● Add a sweeper.
● Allow the feeders to be a part of the attack.

PART V:
Small Games

Section A.
1 v 1 Drills

DRILL #70
3/4 FIELD WITH 1 v 1

Emphasis: Individual defense, beating an opponent for a shot on goal, individual transition from offense to defense.

Formation:

→ Pass
〜► Dribble

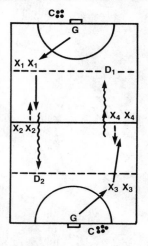

Procedure:
- GK clears ball to X_3 and X_1.
- X_3 passes to X_4 (moving to receive the ball).
  X_1 passes to X_2 (moving to receive the ball).
- X_4 plays 1 v 1 against D_1.
  X_2 plays 1 v 1 against D_2.
- The defensive player clears the ball from C to the line on the right and goes behind the line she passed the ball too. The offensive player sprints to the opposite striking area to become the new defender.

Note: The offensive player after completing the 1 v 1 situation must sprint to become the new defender. The defender is responsible for clearing the ball to start the new attack.

DRILL #71
RAPID FIRE DEFENSE

Emphasis: Offense - ball control.

Defense - timing and control of tackles, tackling in retreat, recovering.

Formation:

A - Attack
D - Defense

～～► Dribble

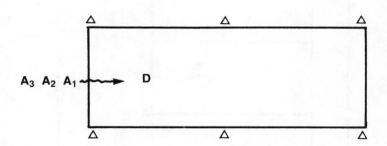

Procedure: One player begins as defense inside the 7' x 15' playing area and goes 1 v 1 with each attacking player. If D gains possession of the ball, she dribbles the ball back to the starting line and leaves the ball. She picks up the next attacking player. If A_1 takes the ball all the way through, D runs quickly to the starting line to pick up A_2. She continues until she has gone against all of the attacking players. If either player goes outside of the playing area to play the ball, stop the play and start again at that spot. Rotate a new D.

DRILL #72
GETTING BACK

Emphasis: Defensive player works on recovering after being beaten by the offensive player.

Formation:

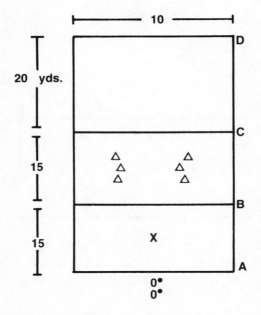

Procedure: O - The offensive player tries to get the ball across line B. If successful she quickly moves the ball in and out of either set of cones and tries to get the ball across line D.

X - The defensive player if beaten in the first grid A to B must run back quickly and be ready to go 1 v 1 again in the grid C to D. Whenever the defense gets possession of the ball, she must cross either line C or A to win the confrontation. The defensive player stays in until she has gone against three to four offensive players.

DRILL #73
WALL TAG

Emphasis: Ball control, conditioning.

Formation:

~~➤ Dribble   • Ball

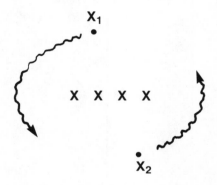

Procedure: X_1 is "it". On the whistle, X_1 dribbles around the wall chasing X_2. If she catches and tags X_2, X_2 becomes "it". Players can move in either direction around the wall. At the end of forty-five seconds, X_1 and X_2 switch with the other players from the wall. Repeat until all six have gone.

Variation: • Divide the wall in half to give the two players another option

DRILL #74
FACE OFF

Emphasis: Concentrate on maintaining control of the ball without fouling.

Formation:

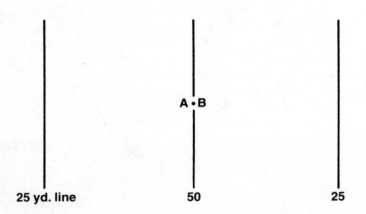

25 yd. line   **50**   **25**

Procedure: On the whistle each player tries to get clear possession of the ball. Continue play as the loser tries to get possession of the ball before her opponent reaches the boundary line. Play periods can be three minutes or longer.

DRILL #75
1 v 1 WITH GOALS

Emphasis: Scoring and conditioning.

Formation: Six players would be an ideal number to work with on this drill. Two players are involved in 1 v 1; two players are the goals and stand with their legs apart; two players are resting. The goals are twenty yards apart. Have five balls available.

Procedure: Players involved in the 1 v 1 play for one minute. Goals are scored by putting the ball between the legs. If a goal is scored, the same person remains on attack and takes one of the extra balls by the goal and immediately tries to score at the opposite goal. If the defense gets possession of the ball, she then goes on the attack.
Example of rotation after one minute of play:
- 1 v 2, 3 and 4 are goals, 5 and 6 rest.
- 3 v 4, 5 and 6 are goals, 1 and 2 rest.
- 5 v 6, 1 and 2 are goals, 3 and 4 rest.

DRILL #76
TACKLE BOX

Emphasis: Offense - maintaining possession of ball.
Defense- capitalizing on mistakes, tackling.

Formation:

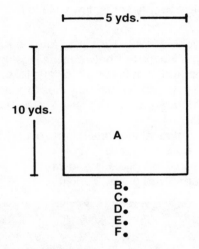

Procedure: Player A stands in the middle of the box. The remaining players each with a ball stand in line ready for their turn. On signal, player B tries to beat player A and control the ball over the end line. Player A tries to tackle player B and after gaining possession, she passes the ball over the boundary line for the 1 v 1 to end. Next offensive player goes in. Players A remains in the middle for a two minute period. Rotate another player in to play defense. Players call their own fouls.

Variation: ● Use a point system: 1 point for the defense if they stop the attack; 1 point for the offense if they get the ball over the opposite line.

DRILL #77
CHALLENGE

Emphasis: Offense - 1 v 1 beating the opponent to the left.
Defense - tackling and forcing the offense to the right.

Formation:

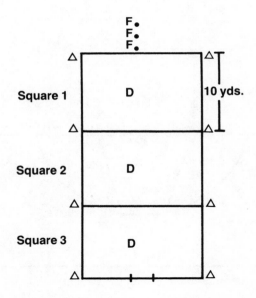

Procedure: Forwards begin by entering square one. Forwards try to pull the defense to their right and beat them on the left. If the forwards win, they go to square two and if successful, go on to square three and eventually getting a shot on goal. The defense attempts to keep the forward on her right and make the tackle. If the defense gains possession, she clears the ball between the two side cones.

Note: As soon as one forward has progressed to the next square, another one begins in square one.

DRILL #78
POSSESSION

Emphasis: Speedwork, shot toward goal.

Formation:

---► Movement w/o ball

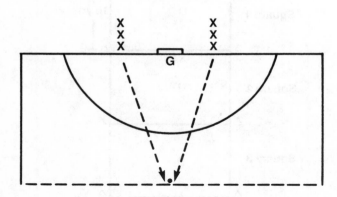

Procedure: The ball is placed on the twenty-five yard line. On the whistle a player from each side of the goal sprints out to the ball. The first player who gains possession attempts to get a shot at goal. The player who did not gain possession becomes the defender.

DRILL #79
RECEIVE AND BEAT THE "D"

Emphasis: Dodging, receiving from behind, shooting.

Formation:

G - Goalkeeper
D - Defense
F - Forward
L₁ L₂ - Links

~~~► Dribble
——► Pass
– – ► Movement w/o ball

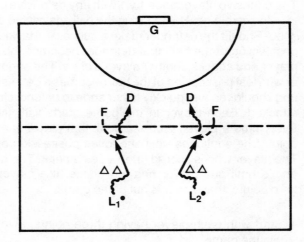

Procedure: The link L₁ or L₂ practice a variety of dodges around the cones. Once the dodge is made, she gives a pass to the forward who must cut back to the ball. Once she has possession, she goes 1 v 1 with the D. Play continues until a goal is scored or the ball is hit outside of the circle.

Variation: • Add cones which the forward must weave in and out of before meeting the D.

DRILL #80
SHOES

Emphasis: Development of both offensive and defensive 1 v 1 skills.

Formation: Use three to six players.

For each player participating in this drill, a shoe (cone) is needed for use as a goal. Place the shoes at equal intervals around the perimeter of a circle (approximately twenty yards in diameter). Each player will have a shoe to defend.

Procedure: One player starts with a ball and is on offense. All other players are on defense and each defends her goal (shoe). The offensive player goes 1 v 1 with any defensive player and tries to score a goal by touching the ball against the defender's shoe. Should the defender make a successful tackle and gain possession of the ball, that defender becomes the offensive player and attacks another player's shoe. The offensive player who lost possession of the ball becomes a defensive player and should recover quickly to her shoe to defend it from being attacked. Each player in the game starts with five points. Every time a player scores a goal, that player is awarded a point. She continues until she loses possession of the ball. The player who is scored upon loses a point. The game continues until one player has ten points. If a player reaches zero points, that player is out of the game.

Variation: • Start with each player having three points. Five points to win the game.

DRILL #81
TACKLING BOXES

Emphasis: 1 v 1 skills.

Formation:

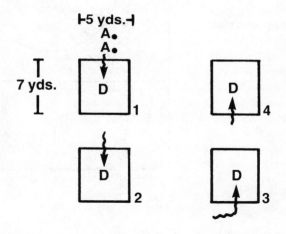

Procedure: Attacker dribbles into the box and tries to beat the defender. If the attacker is successful, she continues on to the next box. If she is unsuccessful, she still continues on the next box. The defense concentrates on jabs and containment before making the tackle.

DRILL #82
BEST WISHES FOR A
SPEEDY RECOVERY

Emphasis: To increase defensive quickness in transition from attack to defense.

Formation:

G - Goalkeeper
D - Defense
F - Forward
-- -▸ Movement w/o ball
——▸ Pass
〉〉〉〉 Shot
⌁⌁⌁▸ Dribble

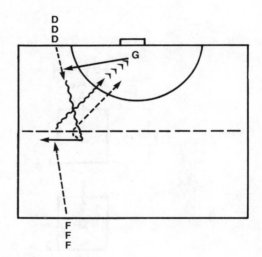

Procedure: Drill begins with the goalkeeper clearing to her right. The defender collects the ball and accelerates up field beyond the twenty-five yard line. She gives a flat pass to the outside. A forward moving at top speed intercepts and goes to goal for the shot. The defender must pivot and recover toward goal to tackle in retreat while forcing the attack to the outside. This drill may be begun with a shot from Jugs (Ball machine) or feeder to give the goalkeeper better practice. Be sure to position well out of the way of the retreating defender.

Variation: • Work from other side of the field. The goalie clears left. Stress recovering to the inside, goal side.

94

Section B.
2 v 1 Drills

DRILL #83
TRANSITION

Emphasis: Quick transition.

Formation:

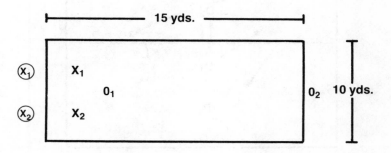

Procedure: Constant 2 v 1 play. X_1 and X_2 go against O_1. If the X's make it to the end line, they immediately go the other direction against X_1. If X_1 gets the ball away from her opponents, X_2 immediately joins her and goes against defender O_1 or O_2.

Variation: • Limit time or vary size of the area.

DRILL #84
FIND THE FREE ATTACKER

Emphasis: Pressure fielding of the ball and initiating attack play.

Formation:

G - Goalkeeper
A - Offense
D - Defense

⟶ Pass
--→ Movement w/o ball
〜➤ Dribble

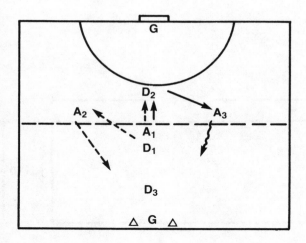

Procedure: A_1 hits the ball to D_2 and rushes at speed towards D_2. D_1 moves towards A_3 or A_2. D_2 passes to A_2 or A_3 depending on the direction D_1 moves. A_2 and A_3 join to play 2 v 1 against D_3.

Variation:
- 2 v 2 - D_1 stays with either A_2 or A_3 and D_3 picks up the free attacker.
- 3 v 2 - A_1 joins the attack.
- 3 v 3 - D_2 joins the defense.

96

DRILL #85
SCORING TURKEYS

Emphasis: Offense - getting free to make a shot at goal.
              Defense - intercepting or getting in a positive tackling position.

Formation:

  G - Goalkeeper   ➝ Pass
  --➤ Movement w/o ball   〰➤ Dribble

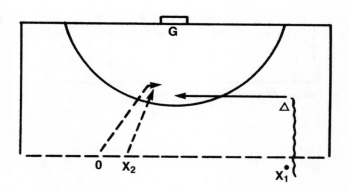

Procedure: X_1 dribbles to the cone and passes anytime thereafter to X_2. O tries to intercept or make the tackle if X_2 gets the ball. O may take off anytime X_2 does.

Variation: • X_1 can become available for a return pass, but she may not score.

97

DRILL #86
2 v 1

Emphasis: Ball control and teamwork in close spaces.

Formation:

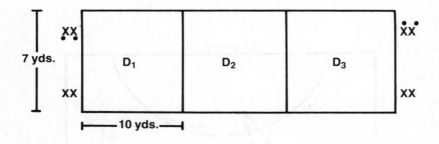

Procedure: A pair of X's attempt to work the ball through boxes 1, 2, 3. D_1, D_2, and D_3 may only tackle in their own box. X's get a point for every box they successfully pass through with possession of the ball. D's get a point for every ball they carry in to the next box or opposite line. Alternate attack from the opposite side. Change D's every three to five minutes.

Variation: ● No dribbling.
● Only dribbling and use of the flat pass.

DRILL #87
MORE WAYS THAN ONE

Emphasis: Defense - Marking, taking way the "give and go".
Offense - Creating an attack.

Formation:

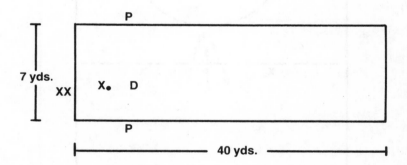

Procedure: X tries to beat the defense by either going 1 v 1 or by using either P_1 or P_2 to create the "give and go". P_1 and P_2 may run along the side line and may only pass. They may pass to one another. They must recognize when to pass to X in order to make the "give and go" work. They must also recognize when **not** to pass to X should the defense be marking well. They need to allow X to cut back and allow her to start another attacking scheme. If X beats the D, the next X begins. The D stays in for two to four minutes.

DRILL #88
COOL CUCUMBER

Emphasis: Receiving under pressure, passing under pressure, transition.

Formation:

  G - Goalkeeper

—–➤ Movement w/o ball

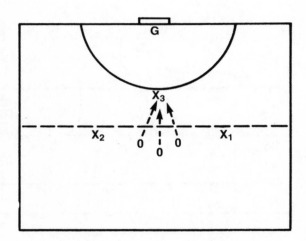

Procedure: X_1 hits the ball hard to X_3 who must quickly pass to X_1 or X_2. The O's try to gain possession and if they are successful, attempt to score.

Variation:
- Alternate the direction of the hit from X_1 to X_2.
- Continue the play so that the drill becomes a 3 v 3.

DRILL #89
DEFENSE RECOVERING

Emphasis: Defense - recovery, pressure cover, communication and conditioning.
Offense - fast break.

Formation:

D - Defense 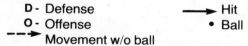 → Hit
O - Offense • Ball
‐‐‐► Movement w/o ball

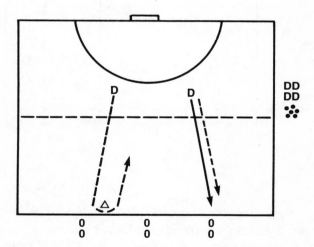

Procedure: Defense hits the ball towards three offensive players who will try to score while the other defensive player runs up around the cone and back to a recovering position. The drill will be 3 v 1 until the other defender recovers, thus making it 3 v 2. If the defense intercepts the ball, they carry or hit the ball across the fifty yard line. Then the new defense will rotate in. The new offensive line also rotates in to start the procedure over again. Extra balls should be beside the defensive line.

DRILL #90
BASIC SQUARE

Emphasis: Attack - support around the ball.
Defense - pressure on the ball, cover through pass.

Formation:

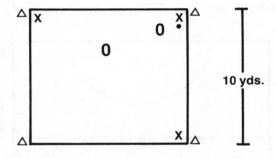

Procedure: X's pass the ball and must move so that they maintain support around the ball. O's pressure the ball and cover so that the through pass is denied. Communication is important with the defense. X's get a point for a through ball and for the number of consecutive passes. O's get a point for an interception.

Variation:
- Start with one defender. Defender stays in for 1 to 1-1/2 minutes.
- Add another defender.

DRILL #91
CAPITALIZE

Emphasis: Putting pressure on the ball, taking away the options, transition.

Formation:

▲ ▲ Goals

▲
▲ Side line
▲

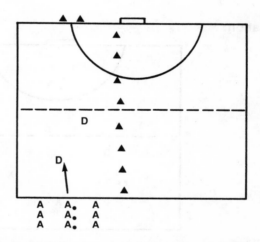

Procedure: Play always begins with the middle attacking player hitting the ball very hard to the first defensive player who is standing approximately seven yards away. How the defensive player fields the ball will dictate what the other players will do. If the defensive player stops the ball dead on her stick, she tries to pass the ball across the fifty yard line. The attacking players try to block the passing lanes and try to prevent the ball from crossing the line. If the attack is successful, they immediately go on attack and with speed try to score against the two defensive players. If the defensive player on the initial hit does not field the ball well, the attacking players go for the rebound or put pressure. The other defensive player tries to give support. The attacking players want to maintain the pressure and eventually capitalize on a defensive mistake. Once the ball goes out of bounds the next set of attacking players begin. Change defensive players after four to six attacking sets.

DRILL #92
REVOLVING TRIANGLE v
TWO DEFENSIVE PLAYERS

Emphasis: Spatial and player awareness, use of depth and width in support, movement off the ball, transition.

Formation:

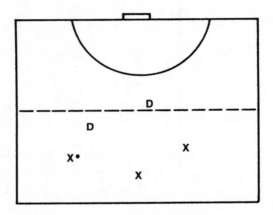

Procedure: Offense - must never be in a straight line and must move out of their starting positions as they progress down field.

Defense - one must commit as the pressure player depending on the ball side. The other defensive player drops back as the cover. Switch roles whenever the penetrating pass occurs or the pressure player gets beaten.

Objective - the offense tries to create the opportunities and eventually tries to get a shot at goal. The defense concentrates on putting constant pressure. If they gain possession of the ball, they must complete two passes to end the play.

Variation: Progression:
- Offense only.
- One defense.
- Two Defense.

DRILL #93
MARKING

Emphasis: Marking.

Formation:

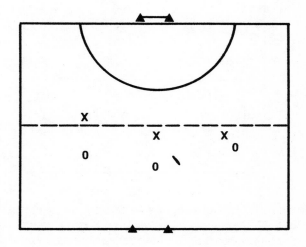

Procedure: Use a frisbee. One team starts with possession of the frisbee. The defense concentrates on marking, frisbee side, goal side. After catching the frisbee the player may only take two steps. The defender must back away five yards and attempt to position for an interception or knock down. Goals are scored by throwing the frisbee into the designated goals.

Variation: ● Add more players.

DRILL #94
SCATTER HOCKEY

Emphasis: Marking, recognizing open space and utilizing it, giving support, putting pressure on the ball.

Formation: Playing area is approximately 30 yds. x 30 yds. Goals are two feet apart.

△ △ Goals

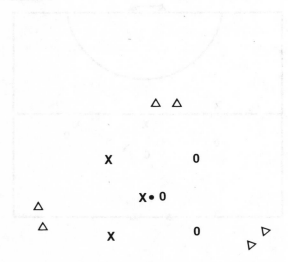

Procedure: Determine 3 v 3 teams. Start with a bully to establish possession. The object is to score points by passing the ball through the cones to a teammate. After scoring a point through one set of goals, the team must move on to another goal. The game is over after a determined playing period.

Section D.
4 v 2, 4 v 4, 5 v 2, 5 v 3, 6 v 2 Drills

DRILL #95
FULL FIELD 4 v 2

Emphasis: Offense - passing skills, off the ball movement, shooting.
Defense - pressure, cover concept, recovering, outlet passing.

Formation:

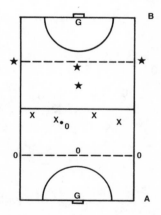

Procedure: X's start with the ball and attack A's end. The two O's defend. Play continues until X scores or hits the ball out of bounds or the defensive players intercept the ball and send it to their wings. Then O's go on the attack towards B's end where the *'s are defending. Procedure is repeated. When the *'s get the ball, they will then be attacking A's end with X's defending. This is a continuous drill. Defensive players must have possession of the ball for three seconds before they can go on attack. Wings must stay flat with the ball.

DRILL #96
LOOK FOR LOONIES

Emphasis: Support on attack, finding free teammate, changing field of play.

Formation: Two teams of four players. The goals are two yards wide.
1/2 a field is used.
▲ ▲ Goals.

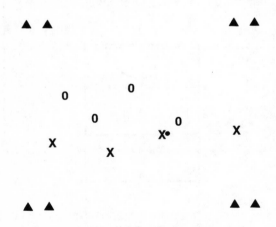

Procedure: One team is given possession of the ball. A team tries to score
by passing the ball through the cones to a teammate. A team
may choose to use any set of goals.

DRILL #97
5 v 2

Emphasis: Recognize numerical superiority, transition of offense to defense, communication.

Formation:

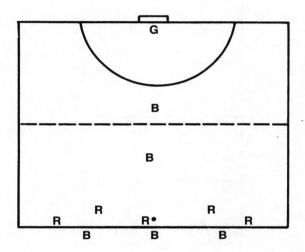

Procedure: Five red start from the fifty yard line against two blue defense. The rest of the blue team are at the fifty yard line and at the start must do three push ups and three sit ups. When they finish, they can join their defense to try and get possession of the ball. If the blue gains possession, red team must send three players back to the fifty yard line to begin their sit ups and push ups. After each change in possession, the attacking team must start from the fifty yard line.

Variation: ● Change the push ups and sit ups to air dribbling, etc.

DRILL #98
5 v 3 and 1 v 1

Emphasis: 1 v 1 skills, defensive team work.

Formation:

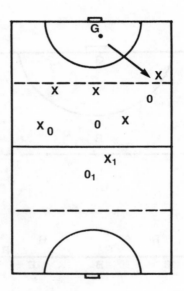

Procedure: Play begins with a clear from the goalkeeper. The defense (X) work the ball out to X_1 who then goes 1 v 1 with O_1. If O_1 gets possession of the ball, she tries to pass the ball to one of the attacking O players. The players may not cross the fifty yard line. 1 v 1 players are in for one to two minutes. 3 v 5 players are in for five to ten minutes.

Variation: • Add another 1 v 1 set so that there is a 2 v 2 situation.
• Allow the closest defending X to join the attack so that it becomes 2 v 1.

110

DRILL #99
5 v 3

Emphasis: Creation of fast break, use of overload, defense repositioning and pressuring.

Formation:

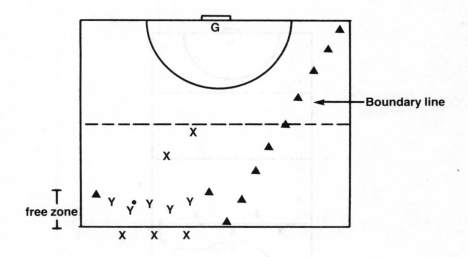

Procedure: Y's have the ball in the free zone. X's cannot enter the free zone. They position to put pressure and to cover. Three X's sit behind the free zone with their backs to the play. Y's can leave free zone when the ball is moved from the zone. X's then call for help and the three X's who were sitting join their teammates on defense. If X's gain possession, they must work the ball into the free zone at which point three Y's must go behind the free zone and sit with their backs to the play. All X's must be in the free zone at the same time before the play can restart.

111

DRILL #100
WORK AT SPEED

Emphasis: Working the ball the length of the field as fast as possible.

Formation:

X- Offense
0- Defense

--- ➤ Movement w/o ball
⟶ Pass

Procedure: One of the defensive players begins the drill by passing a flat pass out to the outside forward. Once the defensive player hits the ball, she immediately helps the other defensive player to contain the attack. The attack tries to get the ball to the opposite end as fast as possible and get a shot at goal. Once the ball goes out of bounds or a goal is scored the drill is done going the opposite direction. If the defense gets possession of the ball, they must try to hit the ball over the end line. Change the defense after four lengths of the task.

112